OXFORD
UNIVERSITY PRESS

Great Clarendon Street, Oxford, OX2 6DP,
United Kingdom

Oxford University Press is a department of the University of Oxford. It furthers the University's objective of excellence in research, scholarship, and education by publishing worldwide. Oxford is a registered trade mark of Oxford University Press in the UK and in certain other countries

Text © Oxford University Press 2023

The moral rights of the author have been asserted

First Edition published in 2023

All rights reserved. No part of this publication may be reproduced, stored in a retrieval system, or transmitted, in any form or by any means, without the prior permission in writing of Oxford University Press, or as expressly permitted by law, by licence or under terms agreed with the appropriate reprographics rights organization. Enquiries concerning reproduction outside the scope of the above should be sent to the Rights Department, Oxford University Press, at the address above.

You must not circulate this work in any other form and you must impose this same condition on any acquirer

British Library Cataloguing in Publication Data

Data available

ISBN: 978-1-382-04350-2

10 9 8 7 6 5 4 3 2

The manufacturing process conforms to the environmental regulations of the country of origin.

Printed in China by Golden Cup

Acknowledgements

The Great Cake Construction and *Record-breaking Food* written by Marcus and Shareen Wilkinson.

Content on pages 10, 41 and 42 written by Suzy Ditchburn

Illustrated by Amy Jindra, Pauline Gregory and Q2A Media Services Pvt Ltd

Author photos courtesy of Shareen Wilkinson.

The publisher and authors would like to thank the following for permission to use photographs and other copyright material:

Photos: Cover: Stoliarova Daria / Shutterstock; Milkovasa / Shutterstock; p44: vitals / Shutterstock; p45: Milkovasa / Shutterstock; p48: PJR-Photography / Shutterstock; p49(t): Irina Buu / Shutterstock; p49(b): Susan B Sheldon / Shutterstock; p50: AlamyRobert Davis / Alamy Stock Photo; p53(bkg): gregl87 / Shutterstock; p53: Sara Winter / Shutterstock; p55: CJLWS / Alamy Stock Photo; p56(t): Victoria Sergeeva / Shutterstock; p56(b): Joe Gough / Shutterstock; p58: Marco Scisetti / Shutterstock; p60: Hortimages / Shutterstock; p61: tatianamelnik / Shutterstock; p62: Mironov Vladimir / Shutterstock; p64: vincenzo de bernardo / Alamy Stock Photo; p65: Imaginechina Limited / Alamy Stock Photo; p66: DustyDingo / Alamy Stock Photo; p67: Jim West / Alamy Stock Photo; p68(a): AlamyRobert Davis / Alamy Stock Photo; p68(b): CJLWS / Alamy Stock Photo; p68(c): Joe Gough / Shutterstock; p68(d): Hortimages / Shutterstock; p68(e): Imaginechina Limited / Alamy Stock Photo; p68(f): Jim West / Alamy Stock Photo; p68(g): Mironov Vladimir / Shutterstock; p68(h): gregl87 / Shutterstock; p68(i): DustyDingo / Alamy Stock Photo; p68(j): vincenzo de bernardo / Alamy Stock Photo; p68(k): Marco Scisetti / Shutterstock; p69(t): Hortimages / Shutterstock; p69: vitals / Shutterstock.

Every effort has been made to contact copyright holders of material reproduced in this book. Any omissions will be rectified in subsequent printings if notice is given to the publisher.

MIX
Paper | Supporting responsible forestry
FSC™ C110497

In this book ...

The Great Cake Construction.......... 11

Record-breaking Food 43

Have a go!

al as in half

augh as in caught

ss as in mission

si as in illusion

ti as in scrumptious

ci as in optician

Read this book if ...
YOU LOVE BAKING, WORKING AS A TEAM AND RECORD-BREAKING FACTS!

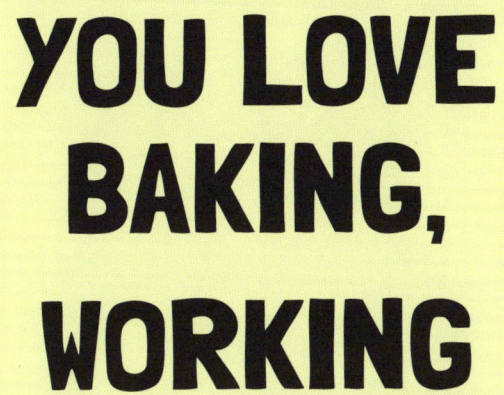

9

In this book, a group
of children aim to make
a record-breaking cake!

**STOP
AND
THINK**

What sort of cake would you
make for the competition?

THE GREAT CAKE CONSTRUCTION

Written by Marcus Wilkinson
and Shareen Wilkinson
Illustrated by Amy Jindra

Isabel

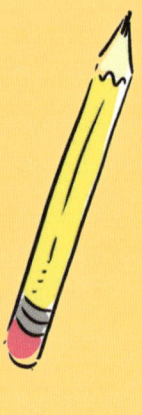

Mrs Henry

Finley

Arnav

It seemed like any other ordinary day. Then Mrs Henry made a **special** announcement.

All the children paid attention as Mrs Henry spoke. The class had been entered into a **record-breaking** cake competition!

The class looked at each other in **amazement**. They were going to make the world's **BIGGEST** cake.
It was going to be scrumptious.

The children had visions of
eating cake and
winning records.

They had just **two weeks** to make the cake!

The children made suggestions.

"Could we make a **dolphin-shaped** cake?" Finley asked.

Mrs Henry explained it must be a round shape. "This will help make it stable," she said.

Then the class voted on what sort of cake was **best**. It was a **hard** decision.

In the end, **vanilla sponge** was the winner!

The children were **eager** to get started. However, Mrs Henry asked them to be patient.

"First, we must make a plan," she said.

Mrs Henry showed some ways to construct the cake. The children **gasped**.

How can we make it that **big**?

It was like constructing a **tower!**
The cake would be made from lots of
sections of
smaller cakes.

At the next session, it was time to start baking!

The next morning, there was a **problem**. Mrs Henry had come to school with her pet hamster, Precious ... but Precious had **ESCAPED!**

A trail of crumbs led to the naughty hamster's location. Precious had eaten the cake! The children would have to start **ALL OVER AGAIN**.

Isabel was **distraught**. "What can we do now?" she wailed.

James stayed calm. "We can do this if we work together," he said.

After lots of sessions, the cake looked **fantastic**.

"It must be almost finished," said Finley. He opened the window. It was **hot** after all the baking.

"Congratulations, team!

We have one sponge left to finish," beamed Mrs Henry.

Isabel had mixed some icing for the last layer. She put the leftover icing on the side.

Suddenly, a *gust* of wind swept in from the open window.
It blew the bowl off the side!
It made an **atrocious** mess.

splat!

"Yuck!" said Arnav.
"We'd better clean up this mess.
The judges will not be impressed."

"At least it's a *delicious* mess!" sniggered Isabel. She licked icing off her finger.

The next day, the children finished the **gigantic** cake.

It looked magnificent. The tower of cake reached as **high** as the roof.

I can't believe how **big** it is!

The final job was to put the **cherry** on top! Now, everybody had to wait for the judges to arrive.

When the judges arrived, they checked the cake's **height**. They checked it was stable. They even tasted it.

The judges's discussions took a **long** time. Everybody felt nervous.

The head judge made a speech.

"Congratulations! You are the official world record holders!"

"This is the **largest** cake ever made by children," the judge continued. "You have shown great baking skills!"

Everyone **cheered!**

"This is the best day of my life," said Isabel.

The school won a **gold cup**. The children got in line to have their photo taken.

Finally, everybody got to eat the cake. It was *delicious*. Even Precious was allowed a few crumbs!

Look back

1. Why did the cake have to be round?

2. Explain what the word 'distraught' means.

3. How did they put a cherry on top of the cake?

In this book, you will find out about record-breaking foods!

STOP AND THINK

How do you become a world record-breaker?

RECORD-BREAKING FOOD

Written by Marcus Wilkinson and Shareen Wilkinson

Illustrated by Pauline Gregory

Contents

World record foods 44
How do you get a world record? 46
Tallest cupcake tower 50
The biggest pumpkin 52
Amazing ice creams 54
Fish and chips 56
The largest lemon 58
Hot, hot, hot! 60
Noodle soup 62
Longest foods 64
Funny food records 66
Glossary and Index 69

World record foods

Would you like to eat the world's **tallest** ice cream?

How about feasting on the **biggest** bowl of **noodle** soup?

A world record means something is the best in the world. It must be **bigger** or *better* than anything else.

> There are many foods that hold a world record!

How do you get a world record?

A special judge checks if a record has been broken.

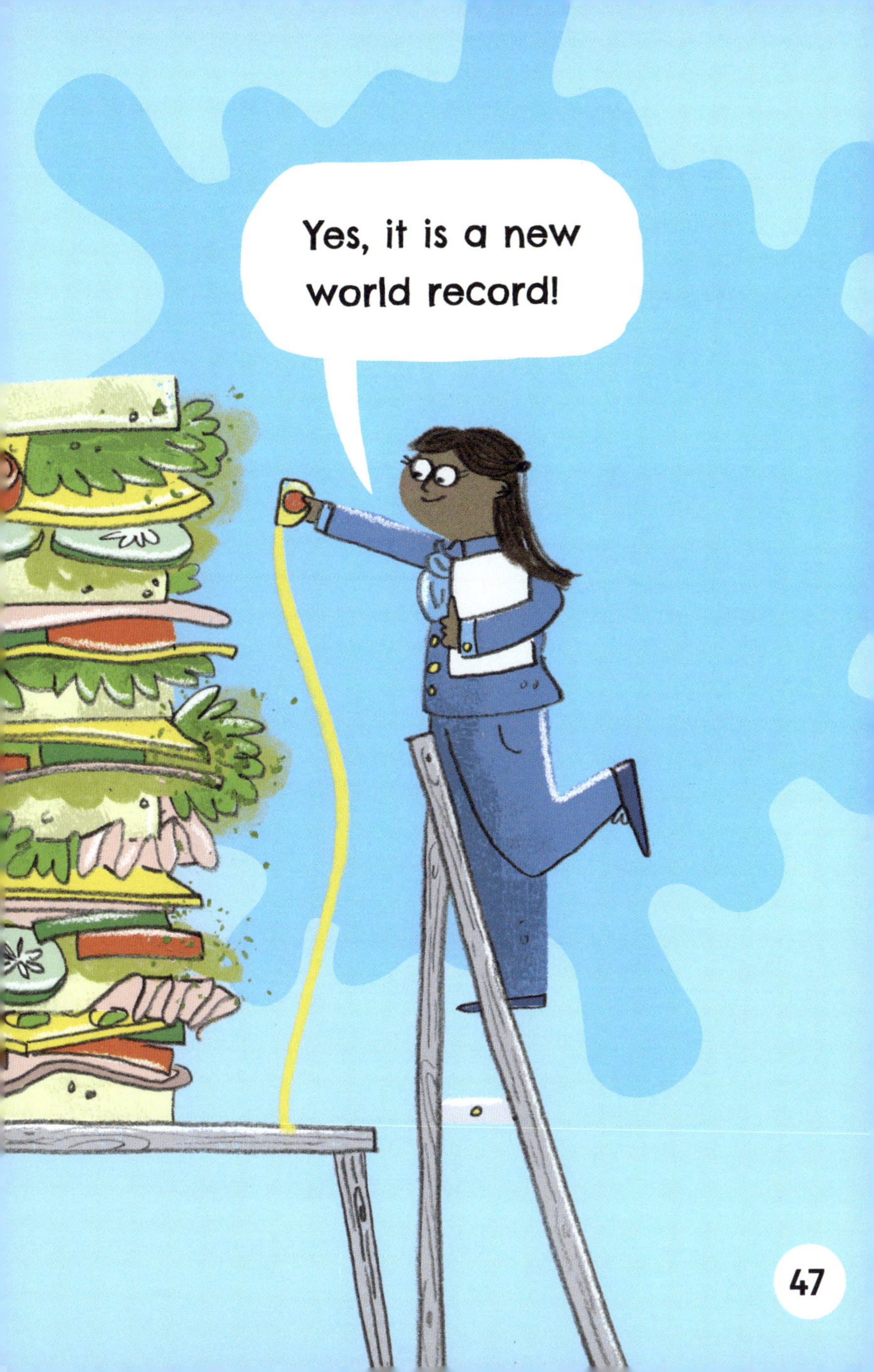
Yes, it is a new world record!

A world record must be able to be broken by someone else. To break a world record, an official judge must record it.

count

A judge must count these **artichokes**. What a mission!

It must be something they can count, **observe** or weigh.

observe

weigh

Tallest cupcake tower

This **tall** tower of **cupcakes** broke a world record. It was made for a special celebration.

The chefs baked 7500 cupcakes!

It was **gigantic!**

The tower was taller than you!

The biggest pumpkin

A pumpkin grown in Italy broke a world record. It weighed 1226 kilograms. This is almost the same as four

GRIZZLY BEARS!

Many people make sweet pies out of pumpkins.

How many pies could you make from such a **big** pumpkin?

Amazing ice creams

How many scoops could you fit on an ice cream cone? One man balanced 125 ice cream scoops on a single cone!

He has a real skill!

This ice cream was made by a chef. It weighed about 450 kilograms!

That is half the weight of a small car!

Fish and chips

A portion of fish and chips also broke a world record.

The chefs used a **giant** fish called a halibut.

That sounds scrumptious!

The **huge** meal weighed almost 50 kilograms.

That's about as **heavy** as ten cats!

The largest lemon

Lemons are often quite small. However, one record-breaking lemon weighed over 5 kilograms.

It was even **bigger** than this.

The lemon weighed about the same as eight basketballs!

Hot, hot, hot!

The world's **HOTTEST** chillies are called Carolina Reapers. They were made by combining two other **HOT** chillies.

You need gloves to hold these chillies. They could **BURN** your skin.

Be cautious!

Noodle soup

One of the **largest** ever portions of noodle soup weighed 1300 kilograms.

It must have been in a **gigantic** bowl!

The noodle soup fed
2000 people.

It weighed the same as three horses!

Longest foods

Look at this dish! It took 250 chefs to make it. They used flour, tomato sauce and cheese.

It was about as long as 56 blue whales.

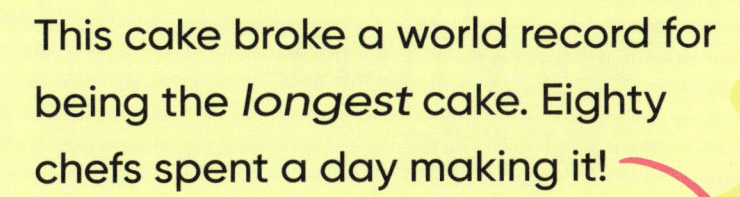

This cake broke a world record for being the *longest* cake. Eighty chefs spent a day making it!

It was the length of about **ten** football pitches!

Funny food records

The record for the *longest* line of canned food is almost 45 000 cans long.

These people are trying to break the record!

This crisp broke a world record. It is on display in a **museum**, so **nobody** eats it.

If you did, it would be like eating 80 normal crisps!

Delicious!

Which record do you think is the most **amazing**?

Glossary

artichoke: a plant which looks like a thistle, parts of which can be eaten

chillies: hot-tasting peppers

cupcake: a small cake baked in a round paper cup

noodle: a thin strip made from flour, water and often eggs

observe: to look at something closely

Index

meals 56–57, 62–64
plants 48–49, 52–53, 58–61
sweet treats 50–51, 53–55, 65

Ha! Ha!

How do you think a banana says thank you?

Thanks a bunch!